Na   ndelstam

MOZART

and

SALIERI

Translated
by
Robert A. McLean

Ardis   Ann Arbor

Nadezhda Mandelstam, *Mozart and Salieri*

Translated by Robert A. McLean

ISBN 088233-034-9 (cloth)
ISBN 088233-035-7 (paper)

Manufactured in the United States of America

TRANSLATOR'S NOTE

The text upon which this translation is based
is essentially identical to that published in the
Vestnik Russkogo Studencheskogo Khristian-
skogo Dvizheniia [Herald of the Russian Stu-
dent Christian Movement] (Paris-New York),
for June 1972. In accord with what it was
felt would be the author's wishes, it has not
been edited with the exception of correcting
obvious misprints and including in footnotes
the Russian from which the English transla-
tions of verse citations were made. I also
added the clarifying subtitle.

Robert A. McLean
Santa Cruz, Spring 1972

CONTENTS

MOZART AND SALIERI

PRELUDES

Mandelstam was a hopeless debater, but he did not bite at just any bait. He loved to tangle with a Marxist although these arguments always went in vain. "They always have a ready answer for everything," he complained after he had wasted time on an empty conversation, convinced that his opponent was simply parrying or avoiding the question, substituting another for it with stunning alacrity. It was easy to draw him into an argument about general philosophical problems, and even easier into a literary duel, chiefly by appraising any phenomena of the current day. He avoided problems of pure literary criticism, leaving them to specialists: "Let them solve them themselves—it is their bread..." In literary criticism he valued good textologists, who had turned out an "intelligent book," i.e. a well prepared edition of some poet (for instance, he liked the one-volume edition of Pushkin), and people excited by poetry like Chukovsky, who, in his opinion, had become the "representative" of Nekrasov, or like Tynyanov with his favorite Kyukhelbeker. But the

9

theoretical works of Tynyanov, Eikhenbaum, and others of *Opoyaz* did not interest him at all. He did not say one word about *Archaists and Innovators,* and when Tynyanov once developed his theory of the two lines of Russian poetry—the "melodic" coming from Zhukovsky, and the other, not unlike the "semantic," the Pushkinian, Mandelstam shrugged it off as a joke. All those models, ladders and frames were not for him. Now I think that in his arguments he defended his literary position, which had its source in his philosophical world view, and that he saw "representatives" simply as readers and "interlocutors" of the poet of the past, and not as purely literary critics.

Akhmatova used to say: "We are all in love with Pushkin," and her love was expressed in her work, her research, her study of texts and secondary materials—in a word, in work that was pure literary criticism. She wrote few articles; only an insignificant part of her ideas and observations went into them or into her "notes." The majority of her discoveries remained unwritten. She came to reject some; others she was too lazy to develop completely and write down, which is a shame, because even in things she renounced (perhaps even especially in these) there was always something the sharp Akhmatova eye had caught. Akhmatova once said that she would probably have written prose if she had not lived in such an accursed era. This is so of course—for prose one must have a table, a drawer, time... Prose has far greater chances of perishing than winged verse. Our life did not dispose one toward prose, and it is easier to resist prose than poetry. And besides the era, which interfered with her writing prose, there were also other reasons, no less important. For example, the enormous difference between her spoken language, which fully reflected the character of her thought, and the way in which she imagined a prose text. Her lively voice and the keenness of her judgments are missing from her written articles. Her thought is moderated, and it is far from being as categorical as it was in her conversation. The fervor and polemical fury which added such inimitable brilliance to her conversation completely disappears. Akhmatova rattled off arguments like bullets, and an enormous amount of preliminary work was necessary to turn a way of thinking and speech

11

such as hers into a prose text. After all, it was not easy to force paper to maintain and transmit to the readers the furious raging of Akhmatova's intonation and thought. This demanded a new form and it simply would not be confined to the standard sort of academic article; and after all, it was into these very letters that Akhmatova was trying to squeeze herself. If she had listened to herself and not been afraid of preserving her voice in a written prose text, we would have been struck by the novelty, force and unexpectedness of this new prose; but work of this kind demands quiet and refusal of any pretense to being in the academic tradition, with its notorious propriety. There was not the slightest hint of quiet in our time, but she herself did not want to violate propriety, besides which in our country people were punished quite severely for this. After all, in poetry, whether you wanted to or not, it was necessary to violate the habitual mustiness of our ideas, i.e., propriety... After all, it was no accident that such a quatrain erupted from her: "For such buffoonery / frankly speaking / a lead pea is all / I could expect from the secretary."[1]

With this kind of perspective was it worth it to listen attentively to one's own voice and, overcoming one's own vacillation and aversions to seek to violate somehow more tactfully the canons of literary criticisms, arguments and proofs?

Everything has its turn; in our country poetry, prose, and all types of essay writing had disappeared, and the only thing that remained for research was the stifled and regulated pseudoacademic article. Akhmatova was not zealous about original prose either, not even about systematically writing down her thoughts about poetry and Pushkin; but she would speak about him a great deal, as the "first poet," and with anyone you pleased, except Mandelstam. It was as if she were restrained around him; but nevertheless at times she would want to know what his feeling was about this or that idea. Mandelstam praised "The Golden Cockerel" (Akhmatova herself later rejected this work) as a well worked out argument, "like a chess game" he said; but he did not express his opinion about the crux of the matter. Knowing how difficult it was to get anything sensible out of him, Akhmatova thought up an original method of fishing for his appraisal. Under the greatest secrecy—God forbid that this should find its way to Pushkin scholars—she explained to me the "plan of the next article," and then, after another day or so, she would ask, "What did Osip say? What does he think?" She had no doubts whatsoever that I would immediately blurt out all her secrets, not only those of her Pushkin criticism, to Mandelstam, even if I had promised a thousand times never to tell anyone... And, furthermore, I knew that this was just what she needed, and I very conscientiously served as the means of transmission.

Once when Akhmatova was visiting us on Furmanov Lane and Mandelstam had gone out for his morning walk (he would get up early and immediately hurry out into the street), I listened to Akhamtova's deliberations about "Mozart and Salieri." Akhmatova wove a thread from the "little tragedy" to the "Egypptian Nights." In her opinion Pushkin was juxtaposing himself to Mickiewicz in these two works. The ease with which Mickiewicz composed was alien to Pushkin, who reproached even Shakespeare for "poor finishing touches." In the "little tragedy" Mozart and Salieri represent two types of composition, and Akhmatova maintained that Mozart seemingly personified Mickiewicz with his spontaneity and that Pushkin identified himself and his work with Salieri. I was very much amazed by this idea: it had always seemed to me that precisely in Mozart I had recognized Pushkin— carefree, idle but such a genius that everything comes to him easily and simply, as if to "God's little bird."[2] Due to academic ignorance we think that "inspired" poetry does not demand the slightest labor, and indeed who, if not Pushkin, is an inspired poet? This is one of the false ideas in the guise of the simplicity and intelligibility of the same Pushkin, which have taken root in us and which exist only in the imagination of lazy readers. Hardly had I stammered "God's little bird," when Akhmatova became furious and maintained that not only did I not know Pushkin, but that I had not even read my own husband Mandelstam. "Did you read the article in *Apollo* about the 'interlocutor'?" (In it Mandelstam expressed doubt that Pushkin had the poet in mind with the phrase "God's little bird": "There are no

15

grounds for thinking that by bird Pushkin meant poet in his song. . . . The bird 'shook its wings and sang' because a 'natural compact' binds it to God, an honor of which a poet of the greatest genius does not dare dream...") At this point Akhmatova took out a sheaf of photographs of Pushkin's rough drafts. They were proof of great, single-minded labor. Mozart, not the historical one, of course, but the one given by Pushkin in the "little tragedy," did not know this labor. Salieri was the vehicle for it.

For corroboration of her idea Akhmatova used "Egyptian Nights." It is common knowledge that Mickiewicz often performed in Moscow salons with his improvisations, demonstrating the ease with which he mastered the flow of poetry. Using this characteristic Akhmatova identified the improvisor of "Egyptian Nights" with Mickiewicz, and even before her Pushkin scholars had noticed a number of features of Pushkin himself in Charsky. Charsky is a man of the world, and poetry is his own personal business, concealed from society and from the idle gossip of literary salons. This, Akhmatova said, is just what the literary position of Pushkin was. (I would say—the one he would have liked to observe). In his mature years, said Akhmatova, Pushkin was very closed, restrained, "buttoned up to the top." He remained inaccessible and cold, as if protecting with armor his guise of "man of the world." (Mandelstam would have expressed the same thought this way: Pushkin regarded the exposed position of the poet in society with disgust, and fighting for the social dignity of the poet, he strictly kept his distance. Mickiewicz conducted himself differently; he was open and trusting, and he appeared in those same salons precisely as a poet. This is borne out by the very fact that he willingly gave "performances" of improvisation; Pushkin, however, would not have given any demonstration of his poetic gift. (it seems to me that the openness of Mickiewicz is explained by the fact that he was a Pole and moved for the most part in Polish circles; and they, it seems, did not kill their poets and at least treated them with respect.)

Thus, Akhmatova wanted to construct her article on the juxtaposition of Mickiewicz (the improvisor of "Egyptian Nights" and the

Mozart of the "little tragedy") to Pushkin (Charsky and Salieri). In corroboration of her words she adduced a few more sorts of proof and material, but Mandelstam did not begin to try to grasp them. After thinking a minute he said, "In every poet there is both a Mozart and a Salieri." This decided the fate of the article; Akhmatova gave up on it.

This was quite casual an episode, and it has no relation whatsoever to Pushkin criticism as it has developed among us. For me the interesting thing in it is the position of Mandelstam, who having written the "Conversation about Dante," took a fresh look at two types of creative process, the representatives of which Pushkin made Mozart and Salieri in his "little tragedy." In his articles from the year 1922 Mandelstam twice repudiated Mozart and extolled Salieri. Furthermore, I consider this instance characteristic also for the "Pushkin criticism of Akhmatova." In her articles Akhmatova pursued her ideas artificially, using the common gambits of literary criticism—in this case she was seeking prototypes. I see in this the symptoms of an illness, widespread among people who are atypical:

they avoid themselves and want to be like everybody else. It is not easy to be oneself and it is very difficult to understand this self; but when one does understand it becomes terrifying—how will people look at this? Will they not be amazed by the trenchancy and unexpectedness of your approach to things which have been much discussed, but not at all the same way you do it... Akhmatova wanted to be a literary critic like everyone else, and she revealed her real, living relationship to poetry and to poets only in her conversations—not in the "plans of her articles" and not in her articles.

The first time I talked with Akhmatova, still in Tsarskoe Selo, I suddenly noticed that she spoke about poets of the past as if they were alive and had only yesterday dropped in on her to read their freshly composed poetry and drink a glass of tea. In reality, Akhmatova, without knowing it herself, was a disciple of Fyodorov. Except that what seemed to Fyodorov the holy duty of descendents (i.e., resurrecting of dead ancestors) became for Akhmatova a natural act of friendship, a living and active relationship of a poet to his forefathers—

friends and brothers in the house of a single
mother, world poetry. It is no accident that
Fyodorov, a child of his century, has much
in common with the materialists. He often
speaks their language; and believing to a
horrifying degree in science, in its limitless
strength and ability to solve all the problems
of life and death, he expects miracles from
it,—precisely worked out methods for the resurrection of the dead. With the help of science
he wants to return to history and into the
present those who have already participated in
the historical drama and passed through that
segment of the historical journey granted
them. After resurrecting all the dead and thus
prevailing over time, in Fyodorov's opinion,
people will enter into a new, apparently extra-
historical stage of existence which will be
something in the nature of the kingdom of
heaven on earth. Fyodorov invented an original variant of Russian chiliasm in which "the
great Slavic dream of the cessation of history"
and the rationalism of the nineteenth century
have been capriciously intertwined. The words
about the "great dream" are taken from
Mandelstam's youthful article "Pyotr Chaa-

daev." He says further, "This is a dream of a spiritual disarmament, after which a certain state called 'peace' will ensue. Not very long ago Tolstoy himself called on mankind to cease the false and unnecessary comedy of history and begin 'to simply live.' " It is no accident that Tolstoy held Fyodorov in such remarkably high esteem... It seems to me that in the very idea of returning all the dead to life on earth (and if there is not enough room on earth, then on the other planets too) there is an indifference not only to history, but also to people. After all, each person does not exist by himself; he is a participant in the great action which is being played out here on earth—in the time and space in which we have been fated to act. What are we going to do when we are returned to earth with the help of Fyodorov's science, in the crush of the generations resurrected since the very creation of the world? We would have to seek out our contemporaries, and would the game be worth the price? Fortunately, the act of resurrection, like the act of creation, is not in the power of science. The stormy development of science in the twentieth century has marked the limits

21

of its possibilities and undermined faith in its omnipotence.

Poets realize Fyodorov's plan in a completely different fashion. Pasternak once said to me about Mandelstam, "He got into a conversation which was started before him." Each poet probably has an intense desire to meet and speak with his predecessors; he has a keen and intensely personal relationship with those whose voices he hears in their living verse, but who are no longer on earth. This is not simply grief at "not meeting" poets from whom they are separated in time, but also a passionate wish to overcome time, to enter into contact with them, in a word, to realize a partial, selective resurrection by an act of love, devotion, and enrapturement... In the "Conversation about Dante" Mandelstam remarks that: "The method Dante selected is anachronistic. And Homer, advancing with a sword dangling on his side—together with Virgil, Horace, and Lucian from the dim shadow of pleasant orphic choruses where this foursome whiles away tearless eternity in literary conversation—is his very best spokesman..." In Tashkent, living in a fair booth,

The Fundamental Prerequisite

In Mandelstam's notebooks there is the entry: "The new literature has made high demands (unfortunately, poorly observed and repeatedly profaned) upon the writer: do not dare describe anything in which the internal state of your spirit is not reflected in some way or other..." That lyric poetry "in some way or other" reflects the inner state of the spirit is something we remember, all the same. As for prose or verse forms which have a greater degree of objectivity, corrupted by narrative literature we see in them the plan, the plot, the design, the ideas (either the author's own or borrowed ones) the so-called devices—everything you would want except the pain and joy of the creator, except his casting about in search of a spark or a moment of inspiration, except what he is asking about, except what it seems to him he has received an answer to. A finished work or a "literality,"[3] as Mandelstam called it, almost never reveals the impulse, the true stimulus for its having been written. The inner theme is always more or less concealed: "Everything

25

is normal: a poem lies there and, as is its nature, is silent. But, suddenly when a theme bursts forth, it begins to knock like a fist on a window..."[4] The understanding of the inner theme, of the fundamental impulse, of that conversation the creator had with himself before he set to work, and of the question torturing him, expands our knowledge of the finished work, reveals its depth.

It is the searching spirit of a man, which prays for a revelation or, rather, for a moment of divine inspiration—after all, the source of art and all kinds of knowledge lies precisely in this. Each true discovery always reflects the inner state of the spirit of one who searched and found, thus leaving an indelible personal imprint on everything that is created or intuited by man. It is just this presence of a personal and spiritual foundation which distinguishes the original from the innumerable surrogates with which the huge, multi-voiced market of art and science is inundated. We do not have the criteria to distinguish the original from the surrogates. As a rule, a clever surrogate seems at first to be a true find, but it is most remarkable that it inevitably dies and does not withstand the test of time, although everything, it would seem, prophesied it a long life. In reality, this "test of time" is as inexplicable as the very creation of the original and its striking persistence. On more than one occasion Akhmatova said to me in amazement, "This poem is not at all what we thought in our youth," and "Who would have thought at the start that the poem would turn out to be so persevering." But Mandelstam, with a flippancy characteristic of him, tried to convince me not to waste my energy in hiding and constantly concealing pieces of paper bearing poetry. "People will preserve them," he would say. I did not want to take that risk; can one depend upon people in general? He would attempt to put my mind at ease, "If they do not preserve them, that means it's not worthwhile." This was an expression of his deep faith in the perseverance of the truth, and considering that a person is not his own judge, he did not want to think about what his poetry was worth. He would have been right had we lived in a normal era when each person lives out his life to his own separate and individual death and poems lie quietly about in desks or in the form of books, awaiting the hour of an unbiased judgment. But in our era of mass destruction and extermination of not only manuscripts but also books, it was I, nevertheless, and not he who was right. After all, up to now almost half a century has passed since these conversations, and the heritage of Akhmatova and Mandelstam has not yet been handed over to the people to judge.

Everyone is already well acquainted with the fact that any portrait is at the same time also a self-portrait of the painter, just as anything with any degree of abstraction is the same portrait, impression, imprint of the spirit and inner form of its creator. This has been pointed out often enough when the question concerned poetry, the most personal form of human activity; but even laws discovered by Einstein or, say, Newton are also portraits of their creators, the breath and warmth of these people on the panes of eternity. V. Vaisberg cited a serious proof against my idea that science has the same personal character as art. He noted that anything of even a second-rate artist is unrepeatable, while a scientific discovery can be made by various people completely independently of each other. I asked I. Gelfand what he thought about this. In his opinion the impersonal appearance of a scientific discovery is explained by the fact that scholars are accustomed—such is the tradition—to providing concentrated and abstracted formulae to what they discover For this reason the results of science are impersonal, and the road to discovery is always individualistic and unrepeatable. And after all, it is really only now that people have begun to be interested not only in the result but also in the path which the scholar has used. It is no accident that almost all the great physicists of our era have left books disclosing their paths and philosophies; and for us as readers, even those who are distant from science, they are no less necessary than the self-confessions of men of art. As for me, I deeply believe that all the forms of man's spiritual activity have one source and one psychic and spiritual basis: man, rather, mankind—"Hagia Sophia with a limitless multitude of eyes"—has been blessed with the cognitive ability, and his higher nature lies in this. And the eyes, sight for

Mandelstam, are the instrument of knowledge. And in this regard every act of cognition, no matter how much it has been prepared by the efforts of the most diverse people, is always accomplished by an individual, the "selected vessel," speaking biblically; and it bears the imprint of his personality.

In poetry each word is a self-confession, each completed work is part of an autobiography. Reading Dostoevsky we do not forget for a minute that this is the confession of a sinner who has laid bare in himself the vices and hopes of his era, and in so doing has seen into the future. The inner state of one's spirit and one's personal principles are the primary conditions for the creation of a literary whole. These conditions are indispensable, although they are by no means the only ones.

No one will doubt that in each work of Pushkin's there are personal principles, something which reflects the inner condition of his spirit. To find this "something" means to penetrate into the primary cause of the creation of the thing, to discover its impetus or hidden inner theme. Akhmatova resurrected Pushkin, once she saw how he languished in anxiety in the flesh, trying to realize what the meaning of his meeting with Mickiewicz was and how the two of them, who lived by poetry and who knew its secrets, went along different paths in their work and in their relations with society. In the finished works, there is no longer either Mickiewicz or Pushkin. There are Mozart and Salieri—two radical manifestations of the creative process; there are Charsky and the wanderer/improvisor, from whose portrait, most probably, all the features similar to Mickiewicz were consciously removed. Is this not why Pushkin did not finish and did not publish "Egyptian Nights"—because Mickiewicz's gift of improvisation and his performances in the salons were still remembered in society? Mickiewicz is not the prototype of Mozart or the improvisor, but meeting the Polish poet could have led Pushkin to the ideas which, once they had taken shape, produced first the "little tragedy," and then, probably in connection with the problems facing Pushkin in Petersburg, the sketch about the improvisor. With her hypothesis about the genesis of these works of Pushkin, Akhmatova did not make a discovery in literary criticism—literary criti-

cism does not concern itself with such things—
but she did uncover Pushkin's original frame
of mind before the idea of the "little tragedy"
formed in him. She exposed the primary basis
of this work.

According to Akhmatova, Pushkin, a-
mazed by the spontaneity in Mickiewicz's
work introduces a type of poet who lives by divine inspiration and calls him Mozart. His own
method of work he gives to Salieri. According
to Mandelstam, Pushkin abstracts the two sides
of creative labor without which no single poet
can manage. The "little tragedy" is a multi-
levelled thing. I. Semenko sees in it the theme
of genius (Mozart) and its divine nature, which
is incompatible with villainy. A genius evokes
envy (as it is commonly known, Pushkin has
an entry about Salieri, the phrase: "An envious
person who was capable of hissing Don Juan
could have poisoned his creator..." This goes
back to one of the legends about the relations between Mozart and Salieri. What de-
serves attention is that this entry was made
already after the "little tragedy" Mozart and
Salieri was written and even published.)

Considering the theme of envy of a

genius the basic theme of the "little tragedy," I. Semenko remarks that Pushkin himself knew that he evoked the envy of many (Katenin, for example, and Yazykov) although he kept silent about it. The following lines of Pushkin prove this: "I hear around myself the buzzing of slander, the verdicts of cunning stupidity, and the whisper of envy and the happy and murderous reproach of flighty vanity ..." She reminds us that Pushkin could have been an unworthy bearer of a gift. Bestuzhev and Zhukovsky wrote Pushkin letters saying how his "genuis" was turned to unworthy subjects... All these reproaches bring to mind point by point the position of Salieri in the "little tragedy." All the arguments of I. Semenko lead to the refutation of Akhmatova's idea of Pushkin's Salierianism.

It seems to me that these points of view are not so irreconcilable. Akhmatova was able to guess the impulse for writing the "little tragedy," and I. Semenko is speaking about a finished work. But I do not think that Pushkin identified himself either with Mozart or with Salieri. Rather, he knew in himself the features of both—both the spontaneity of a

33

gift and work. Any poet knows this, and his rough drafts prove this. My task, however, is not bound up with Pushkinian literary criticism, but only with how Mandelstam understood the two sides of the creative process, which he designated by the words "Mozart" and "Salieri" in his conversation with Akhmatova through me.

The Original Impulse

In his notes to the "Youth of Goethe"
Mandelstam wrote a few words about what he
considered one of the most remarkable poems
of Goethe: "Such things are created seemingly
because people jump up in the middle of the
night in shame and fear because they have
blasphemously experienced so much and not
accomplished anything. Creative insomnia,
despair awakening in a person who sits on his
bed at night in tears, is just as Goethe described
it in his *Meister.* The art of nations moved
because of the   horseman of insomnia, and
where it has trampled there is a place for
poetry or war..."

Most likely, Akhmatova knew this kind
of insomnia too, because after a few years completely independently of Mandelstam, whose
work about Goethe she had not read (it was
a broadcast for the Voronezh radio), these
lines appeared in her work: "Have I not already known all the abysses and paths of insomnia, but this is like a horseman's clatter
to the accompaniment of the howl of a wild
trumpet..."[5] This is a poem of the forties

when the *Poem Without a Hero* had begun to sound in Akhmatova's ears and her every attempt to master it or drown it out failed. Akhmatova would tell how she threw herself into washing laundry and stoking the stove. Although she had always been very lazy about house-work, at such times she was ready for anything if only the anxiety and noise could be removed from her ears. Nothing came of this—the poem got the upper hand of the protesting poet. Evidently it is impossible to suppress such sleepless alarm until it abates by itself, after yielding its place to a state of work. This is the very first stage—seemingly a portent of a ripening poem, most probably like any other creative work.

The question arises: why did Mandelstam bring up war in this entry, and why did a trumpet from a military brass band burst into Akhmatova's poem? Goethe's childhood took place in the period of the Seven Years War, and he often speaks about this in his autobiographical book *Truth and Fiction;* but I do not think that the words about war came to Mandelstam by association: he was nevertheless led by thought rather than association.

And for some reason Akhmatova too understood something connected with war and marches when she began to speak about this insomnia. What is this—an inner mobilization? A signal to assemble for the campaign? An atavistic fear or instinct of war? Mandelstam did not go to war, and Akhmatova only saw people off and cried as is a woman's lot, but nevertheless she sensed the wild trumpet which summoned and drew one to an unknown destination.

According to an unwritten but indisputable law the name of Pushkin was never mentioned among us in the same context as other poets, especially our contemporaries. I was obliged to overcome the inner prohibition, softened only by the fact that I had already mentioned Goethe, in order to say what Pushkin said about that condition which precedes work. He said: "Languishing with a spiritual thirst, in a gloomy desert I lay..."[6] In the past century, of all experiences only love was spoken of openly, and for that matter, usually only being attracted to and falling in love with someone. In order to reveal his own creative experience, Pushkin had recourse to the myth about the prophet; but the sense of the poem is absolutely clear.

Akhmatova called this state "prelyrical anxiety."[7] Such anxiety precedes not each poem, but rather a cycle, a period, a book or, in one manner or another, a whole stage. Moreover, even a separate poem standing isolated from others can evoke an attack of "prelyrical anxiety" before its emergence. Sometimes it seizes a man even in the depths of work, signaling some kind of a displacement, a new course, a turnabout in an inner theme.

The "awakening of despair" or the "prelyrical anxiety" is only the presentiment of the "theme," the expectation of its arrival. I am speaking about the inner theme, and not about what is called the theme in its scholastic sense, i.e., not about the point of departure for subsequent deliberations. The "inner theme" itself does not yet contain any material and has no form as either an argument or a thesis. In the "Conversation about Dante" Mandelstam defines it this way: "At that moment when the necessity for empirical verification of the facts of the legend began to dawn in Dante, when for the first time there

38

appeared in him a taste for what I propose to call holy (in quotation marks) induction, the conception of the *Divine Comedy* was already formed and its success was already internally guaranteed." In this chapter Mandelstam speaks about the *Comedy* as a whole and, in particular, about its third part (but not about the first and more popular part), about the relationship of Dante to biblical cosmogony and to authority, and also about his methods of "verification of legend," which Mandelstam compared to the running of an experiment in modern science.

It is no accident that he says here that the inner theme "began to dawn," i.e., assumed weak and unclear outlines. Pushkin also has told about this moment, recalling how he distinguished the "distant expanse of a free novel" as yet unclear as if through a "magic crystal."[8] In the essay "Word and Culture" Mandelstam has a few words about this earliest stage in the genesis of a poem: "The poem is alive with an inner image, in that resonating impression of the form[9] which anticipates the written poem. There is not one word yet, but the poem already sounds. This is the inner image; this is the poet's hearing touching it."

Mandelstam's definition contains a synthesis of feelings characteristic of him. The "impression" is what is sculpted, what the fingers touched when they sculpted; but he touches this "impression" with his hearing. All five of Mandelstam's senses were well-developed—not only his hearing which was musical and sharp, not only his taste and vision, but also his sense of touch which was almost as strong as a blind man's. Objecting to excessive concreteness he wrote, "Why is it obligatory to touch with one's fingers? A doubting Thomas." But at this point he recalled the blind man, who "knows a dear face barely having touched it with his seeing fingers..." As is commonly known, intellectual tension usually receives motor release—in walking, in the movement of arms or lips. I think that the tension in moments of "pre-lyrical anxiety" resulted in this sharpening of all five senses. After all, in Mandelstam's opinion they are "only vassals, standing in feudal service to an intelligent 'I,' which thinks, which recognizes its own worth..."

40

At this level of creative work the poet is immersed in himself; he listens to himself, to his inner voice. Khodasevich said it well, touchingly complaining that "the heavy spirit of private listening is intolerable for the simple soul—Psyche falls under it..."[10] For Mandelstam this is a period of special quiet. At a conference in Tartu on the psychology of writing poetry, the young doctor Yury Freidin delivered a report based on an adolescent poem by Mandelstam in which this very moment of tense listening is described: "The hearing strains the sensitive sail, the expanded gaze empties, and the flat chorus of midnight birds swims across the silence."[11] Like a whisper the inner voice is quiet, and it is flat like a whisper. (The vocal chords are not included—hence the absence of sonority.)

In Akhmatova this stage would proceed in a slightly different fashion. In the first place, with her, visual images would flash past ("visions of crossed arms"); in the second place, she does not speak about quiet but about a multiplicity of voices she has heard: "It seems" to her "that she hears both complaints and groans of unknown and captive voices," and then "one all-conquering sound" arises from the sounds which are unmixed and not very well differentiated. It is in this, seemingly, that the nature of her gift is manifested: the "one sound" guarantees synonymity and perhaps also the narrative quality of her verse, which almost always develops as a story about one moment. Akhmatova's originality and strength lie in this, and her laconicism results from it.

With Mandelstam this attentive listening is transformed into muttering, and it is not one conquering sound which appears but a rhythmical whole: "How nice it is for me and how burdensome when the moment approaches, and suddenly the stretching of an arch sounds in my mutterings..."[1][2] From this moment the words have already begun to come: "How to transmit this salience and joy when the word smiles at us through tears..."

Judging from these facts the process of creation in its first stage is like this: preliminary anxiety, the resonating impression of form or "mute chorus" vaguely felt by the hearing, the initial muttering in which the rhythmical principle is already apparent and in which the first words come. The anxiety is exchanged for the joy of the first discoveries. But a new misfortune awaits the poet later—searching for a lost word.

In our time, which has liberated self-analysis, by no means Freudian self-analysis but an incomparably deeper and more real kind, two poets who had no connection with each other in any way, who were separated by space and conditions of life, and who spoke in different languages and had not even heard of each other—Eliot and Mandelstam—spoke of the bitter feeling evoked by the loss of a word. This misfortune, common, most likely to every genuine poet, seemingly makes up the "cost of production." The inner voice to which the poet listens carefully is so elusively quiet, that the poet is not always able to catch this elusive word, even by mobilizing all his feelings including his memory: "And memory burns and torments like dark honey on the lips. A word is missing—do not invent it: it sounds by itself, it swings the bell of nocturnal unconsciousness..."[13]

Mandelstam's relation to the word was distinctly expressed in this rough draft: it

43

exists as an absolute reality—in language and tradition—and in a line one must have just that which has slipped away; and one must not replace it with anything else, although as many replacements as you like exist. An invented word or a substitute word is a random event at a time in poetry when everything is regulated by law. On more than one occasion Mandelstam polemicized with both the Symbolists and the Futurists, accusing both the former and the latter of an arbitrary attitude toward the word. It seems to me that the most essential thing in all these conversations is the complaint—"do not invent it"—and the remark in the "Conversation about Dante" about the ineffectual, lexical, purely quantitative nature of word formation. An invented word, even an apt one, even one which has been firmly established in the lexicon, does not change anything in the language other than purely quantitative elements.

Eliot was certainly not obliged to clash with building words from roots, with creating words, or turning words into symbols which were real only in the system of a given poem or given poet; but it is quite likely that if the theme of their poems so coincided, he was like Mandelstam in his understanding of the word.

Most likely this is the consciousness of the correctness and irreplaceability of the word in a poem, and in addition, the understanding of the word as Logos. In Eliot there is coincidence also with Akhmatova, for example, in the poem "But I warn you that I am living for the last time. . ."[14] These coincidences are probably hidden in the ideology of these poets, in their belonging to a Christian culture in a period of very profound crisis which is felt as much in the West as in our country.

It is commonly known that the condition under which the inner voice is heard and the poem is composed does not depend upon the will of the poet—it cannot be summoned artificially. The poet is not master over it as he is over the word. Pushkin spoke about this. Mandelstam knew it from his early youth: "Why is the soul so melodious, when there are so few nice names, and a momentary rhythm is only a chance, even an unexpected Aquilon."[15] The suddenness and unexpectedness of this

Aquilon is its basic feature. But where is its source? In Goethe's poem about the "awakening of despair" it is said that he who has not experienced this condition does not know the forces of heaven either. Is not the condition in which the poet listens attentively to a voice, which is unheard by us and which sounds only in his soul, related to that which is called religious or mystical experience? I have happened to see "the wide-open stare go empty." This is a secret moment into which it is impossible to penetrate, and the little that I have said about it cannot reveal its essence.

A few more words must be said about the originality and inexactness of contemporary terminology. The word "model," which is taken from scientific terminology, is often used today to designate the "resonating whole" which Mandelstam called an "impression," i.e., for the integral poem which still does not exist but which is already in the consciousness of the poet. In science the model of the atom was constructed in this way on the basis of theories explaining its structure. The "resonating impression" is not a model of a poem but the poem itself, as yet undismembered into words, sounds, rhythms, thoughts, and lines. It is not the model of an atom but the atom itself, as also is a finished poem. The relation to an object is different in poetry than it is in science, therefore it is impossible to transfer ideas about nature from science into a science about poetry, if one exists. A poem is a phenomenon created by a poet, and in this phenomenon the subject and the object are inseparable. Studying a finished poem, one can construct as many models as he wishes; but one can superimpose them only on the models of descriptive poetry or on what in poetry lends itself to paraphrasing or dismembering into separate images. And this is the "truest sign of the absence of poetry: because where it is revealed that a thing is commensurate with its paraphrase, no sheets have been rumpled, poetry has not, so to speak, spent the night there..."

The Improvisor

The Mozartian principle seems related to the gift of improvisation only at a superficial glance. The sources of these two types of work are not equivalent, and are perhaps even opposite. Mozart works by living inspiration (in "Conversation about Dante" Mandelstam called this an "impulse").[16] The impulse or divine inspiration accompanies his whole process of creativity. Did not Mandelstam have this in mind when he complained in his adolescent poetry that the "wide wind of Orpheus . . . had gone away into far off lands?" In the "little tragedy" we learn about the peculiarities of Mozart's gift not from him but from the words of Salieri. It is he who testified that the "holy gift" "illuminates the head of a madman, an idle reveler..." It is clear why Mozart is an "idle reveler"—he badly needs relaxation after he has given himself up completely to his "secret hearing." We also know about the evaluation of his work: "You, are a god, Mozart, and you yourself do not know it." The bearer of new and captivating harmony cannot not be frivolous in his hours of leisure, although his is not a vain soul. He could not be vain because his poetic rightness is his inalienable gift. Pushkin, who was also accused of being unworthy of his gift, knew this perfectly well; and the famous poem about the poet weighed down by the "cares of the vain world" was simply a challenge to his accusers and by no means a confession he was forced to make. And how much prattle this poem has engendered—not, by any means, from lovers of work like Salieri, but rather from employers, commissioners, guardians and observers of cultural decorum!... Mozart probably would never have taken the commission of the "black man" if he had not sensed the approach of his own death, and commissioners love to have all lines meet the exact letter of the contract. Mozart was not able to do this because he was not master over this "secret hearing," and it arose not in contractual periods but according to its own unknown laws.

Improvisation has a completely different basis than a lasting impulse. Improvisation is not the inner voice of a poet, not the tense listening to oneself, but work on ready elements, on their elemental combination and adhesion, the deploying of a rhythmical machine possessed by versifiers rather than genuine poets. Mandelstam once heard the proper and sleek Bryusov, the "hero of labor" as the implacable Tsvetaeva called him, improvise in a cafe of poets. He proposed that he be given several themes; he selected one of them, and measuredly, almost without a hitch, before the eyes of the public he composed an average Bryusov poem, put together (in the literal sense of the word) from Bryusov's usual words, unified by the usual rhythm, very correct and somewhat bouncy, and with the usual Bryusov train of thought, which seemed so whimsical and captivating to his contemporaries.

Mandelstam was amazed that this improvised poem of Bryusov's did not significantly differ from those which were collected in his books. Even in Bryusov's improvisation nothing unexpected burst through ("The unexpected is the air of poetry"), and neither did anything accidental or incorrect shine through. Heroes of labor always maintain the standard... The improvised poems seemed just as still-born as everything that Bryusov wrote. "That poem is just like all of his," Mandelstam said, spreading his hands helplessly. He was not amazed by Bryusov's mastery at all (in poetry this is not what is called mastery—on the contrary, it is far from being a sign of a genuine poet, and rather the sign of a translator), but by this entire foolishness: an elderly man finds pleasure in publicly demonstrating how without wasting effort poetry of no use to anyone is composed. The poor improvisor of "Egyptian Nights" resorted to such sterile work only for the sake of money, but Bryusov did it for free or for such small change that one could order only a glass of ersatz tea with a fantastic surrogate pastry. This was in the hungry Moscow of the first years of the revolution when established people such as Bryusov lived on the sale of rags which had been lying around in their apartments, but by no means on their earnings, or even less on their literary honorariums...

I have no doubts that the improvisations of Mickiewicz, the primordial poet, are in no way comparable with Bryusov's. Mickiewicz possessed an incomparably wider keyboard than Bryusov, and the most extensive assortment of poetic elements. This would guarantee a far higher level for an improvised poem, even a whole put together from ready elements. And finally (who knows?), Mickiewicz's nervous structure could have been such that the poetic impulse arose in it suddenly, perhaps even from simple contact with the audience—in a single moment, as when a light bulb flashes on. Something similar, is probably characteristic of actors and born orators—catching fire from contact with the audience. In his Italian improvisor Pushkin depicted not a versifier like Bryusov but a genuine poet—indeed, this is the only respect in which the improvisor of the tale and Mickiewicz have anything in common; in everything else they are radically dissimilar. After all, before he began to improvise the Italian's face underwent a change as if he had felt the "approach of God." Does not every poet await the approach of the "resonating impression of the form" or the impulse in this way? It seems to me exceptionally important that Pushkin, who is a miser when it comes to expressing frankly how creativity issued from him, drew the poetic and mystical experiences together here as if by chance. In one of his most significant books Frank, a remarkable man, a free thinker and a profound philosopher, proves the existence of mystical experience and intercourse with God specifically by analogies with esthetic and ethical experience. I am sure that a poet who has known the nature of "secret hearing" cannot be an atheist. However, he can become an atheist by renouncing his gift or squandering it; only this always ends in tragedy. Indeed, they have renounced their gifts quite often because of both low goals and frivolousness, and most important, because humans lack the spiritual strength, the intellect and moral tenacity for such a severe ordeal. And I would add to Frank's analogy also the experience of scientific intuition and knowledge in general, which one has generally become accustomed to associate only with the reasoning (rational) capabilities of man. In a very similar fashion art is often cut off completely from rational elements, although it cannot exist without them. Both science and art demand all the spiritual capabilities of man —in all their complexity.

Although the improvisor has felt the approach of God, nevertheless in the improvisation of even a genuine poet slips, accidents, voids crammed with worn out elements are inevitable together with the enthusiasms, surprises and knots of vibration. In other words, improvisation consists of isolated flights connected by a unifying cloth of ready-made elements (often narrative because it is easier). The reason for such a structure is understandable: an improvisor, even if it is Mickiewicz himself, does not have the time to listen attentively to himself, to his inner voice. According to the conditions of the game he must not cause the public to become disenchanted due to lengthy pauses. With an improvisor the first stage of the process, the anxiety of awaiting the impulse, is compressed almost to zero—indeed, a momentary process when the "wide-open stare empties" and the inner quiet or "visions of folded arms" advance. Only at moments of the most remarkable concentration can the poet retreat into himself in order to hear the most lofty which has filled him to overflowing, and most likely it is virtually impossible to accomplish this on a stage under the stare of a crowd. Even actors are separated from the auditorium in that it is submerged in semi-darkness. We will permit a brightly lit circus hall only because circus art is the furthest removed from improvisation and secret hearing. It is based purely on craft and a detailed working out of the slightest movements.

Secret hearing is the poet's secret. Pushkin called upon the poet to live alone in order to hide it. The poetic gift does not tolerate vanity; and although the poet is seemingly immersed "in the cares of the vain world" during the periods of interruption, in fact, this is not the way it is at all. No matter how he tries to adjust to people, there is always something alien about him. With both Akhamtova and Mandelstam the interruptions in their writing of verse turned out to be quite lengthy; but even among friends rarely and suddenly a shadow would steal past as if they were checking themselves—to see if something were stirring in their souls. Jovial and sociable in appearance, nevertheless they would suddenly, consciously tear themselves away from their surroundings as if hiding from them. Akhma-

55

tova regulated these states better than Mandelstam; she attempted to hide them so that later she could escape, pretending she was sick. Mandelstam would become estranged even with people present; and once he began to listen to himself attentively, he would suddenly cease hearing what they were saying to him. His passion for walking and strolls—necessarily solitary—answered his need to be simultaneously among people (the passers-by), and alone. Pasternak, who was also a sociable person, who loved to charm and fascinate people, would suddenly become alienated from people, change the whole tone of the conversation, become abrupt and curt. These reversals would seem inexplicable if one did not know the secret necessity of a poet to be tete-a-tete with himself. This by no means means he will begin writing verse at just this moment. In order to begin writing verse one must live and, living, frequently be by one self.

Charsky, as he is presented by Pushkin in "Egyptian Nights," is alienated from people; he erects an invisible partition between himself and the larger society to which he belongs.

His social position, the mask of a man of the world consists of this. But there is also something in his conduct which results from the need of the poet for a certain alienation or distance, as Mandelstam called it. Charsky's relation to society is not accounted for—it is presented as a given. Charsky, reserved and isolated from society, is placed opposite the improvisor not as a poet—we do not even know what he writes and how he works—but only because of his relation to society.

The prose and verse of a poet comprise one whole; but it seems to me the role of secret hearing in the composition of prose pieces is significantly less, and the period of preliminary anxiety is no less acute, than before work on poetry. It seems to me that almost all the prose of poets is knowledge of their inner being and therefore can serve as commentary on poetry. But after all, this is true also for the books of the prose writers of greatest stature—Dostoevsky and Tolstoy... People reared on narrative literature have put out the rumor that the prose of poets is something shaky and of slight significance for the development of prose genres. The further a contemporary literary work recedes from a person's direct speech, as he is frankly or with chaste reticence seeking and discovering himself, the further it is from the prose of a poet.

In spite of the fact that she was truly in love with the first poet, Akhmatova was proud of the fact that she preserved her unbiased nature and knew what things he was weak in and what things he was strong in. Of his prose she placed *Dubrovsky* lowest of all, considering that the work contains the least of all of Pushkin himself. In Akhmatova's opinion, in *Dubrovsky* Pushkin set himself the goal of writing an ordinary tale similar to the literary genres fashionable in his time. In other words, Akhmatova did not see in *Dubrovsky* Pushkin's personal impulse, or his self-portrait, or his knowledge of himself. But all the rest—from his casual remarks to his most consummate works—bears the stamp of Pushkin's personality.

It remains for me to say a few words about a special manner of improvisation that some poets have: impromptu and humorous poetry. These are also built on mastered material—not that of poetry, but that of prose and oral speech; and a true versifier's gift functions by articulating them. In their own way they are very like portraits, because living speech, mischief and laughter have left their imprint on them more than on anything else. In Akhmatova's case the character of the impromptus is somewhat different: they are her quatrains, typically full of bitterness and even jibes. Whatever the epoch is—the poet's impromptu is also.

The Salieri of the Twenties

Mandelstam disassociated himself from Mozart and took Salieri's side unconditionally in two essays of 1922. He admitted their equality only twelve years later, after the "Conversation about Dante" had already been written. Akhmatova has some remarkable lines: "And along the legendary quay the real, not the calendar twentieth century approaches."[17] That the twentieth century did not come immediately when it was supposed to by the calendar but somewhat later, everyone now knows; but some consider that it began with the War of 1914, others with the Civil War. But I think that neither of these wars brought anything at all specifically new with them. The terror and cruelty of war were only a prelude, and the turning point took place at the end of the Civil War, so that in 1922 we stood on the threshold of a new century. Mandelstam knew this and prepared himself for the new life. In the same essay where he says that he is a disciple of Salieri there are a few lines about that former "present." "Everything became heavier and more enormous, and therefore man, too, had to become harder, because a man must be the hardest thing on earth, and he must be to it as a diamond to a pane of glass. The hieratic, i.e., holy character of poetry is conditioned by the conviction that man is the hardest thing in the world." Not even a year had passed when everything became clear, and in the essay "Humanism and Contemporaneity" Mandelstam spoke of man again, but already from a different perspective: faith in the hardness of man had been undermined, and his helplessness compared with the powerful forms of the social structure came into the foreground.

For Mandelstam these were new thoughts and new words. It was clear that some sort of turning point had occurred in him, and it was promoted both by the approach of the real twentieth century and by personal circumstances. In the first place there was the death of Gumilev. In the second, he was no longer living alone but with me, and perhaps he felt responsibility for another person for the first time. One had to feed this person, and in those years this was almost a head-splitting problem. What he thought about Gumilev I found out from scattered sentences and decisions. He firmly decided not to return to Petersburg—the town had suddenly grown empty for him. And he once said that when a group disintegrates an even greater responsibility lies on each person. We found out about Gumilev's death in Tiflis, probably in the middle of September. And a new voice was also heard in one of the poems written in late autumn.

In autumn we lived with B., who had been exiled from Moscow, with whom we often talked about what awaited us. Once trucks rolled up to the buildings where we were living, and within several hours the whole block had been moved. At that time they had already begun to practice mass organized actions such as the moving of a whole block of people or, as once happened in Kiev, a search for the "removal of excess," carried out in one night throughout the whole town. Now after we have experienced the real mass character of these undertakings, it seems like child's play; but still inexperienced at the time, such movings and searches made an impression on us. The first experiences were only a gathering of forces.

The permanent residents of the block were given documents prepared in advance for new lodgings. We had nowhere to go, and our things were thrown onto a small truck; we said "Building of the Arts," and the driver majestically drove us to the assigned place. For some reason or other I recall this phantasmagoria and a most amusing detail which lent a still more fantastic character to everything: the driver was a Negro. Where a Negro came from I do not know, but he whizzed us along the bright central street of Tiflis and stopped by an elegant private residence in the best part of Tiflis. This private residence, abandoned by its owners, was transferred to the ownership of the poets of the "Blue Horns" group, a favorite in Georgia. Arbitrarily, without the permission of the authorities or the "Blue Horns," the new owners of the residence, we took one of the small studies on the lower floor where there were reception rooms, drawing rooms and terraces. On the second floor lived Paolo Yashvili and Titsian Tabidze. Disturbed by our arbitrariness, the servants ran to complain to the commissars of education under whose

63

jurisdiction the residence came; and from time to time, by order of the commissars Kandelaki and Brekhnichev, we were not permitted into the building. On such occasions Yashvili would descend from the upper floor, and waving aside the servant with a feudal gesture, he would let us into the building. We lasted about a month there. The poets gave Mandelstam a translation of Vazha Pshavela, and on the terraces of the lower story from time to time arguments would flare up between them and Mandelstam, into which both sides put their southern fieriness and passion. Mandelstam attacked Symbolism, and Yashvili swore by Andrei Bely's name to annihilate all the enemies of the Symbolists. Mandelstam's anti-Symbolist passion is amply present in all his articles of 1922. The arguments were honed in these disputes in Tiflis. The younger "Blue Horns," Gaprindashvili and Mitsishvili, secretly sympathized with Mandelstam, but the older ones were unyielding. Toward the end Yashvili exclaimed: "Who are you to teach us!" And, after all, he was correct—what kind of mission-ary passion was it that seized Mandelstam so that he attacked what he considered heresy in a poetry foreign and unfamiliar to him. On the other hand everyone agreed on one thing: the evaluation of Vazha Pshavela.

The commissars, convinced that it was impossible to evict us by primitive means (bodily), because of Yashvili's opposition, gave us documents for some hotel with broken windows. We spent a few days there, drank wine with our neighbors, Georgian policemen, and in winter we left through Batum for the north. We greeted the new year 1922 on a steamship in Sukhumi.

The pivotal poem in the new voice, "I bathed at night in the courtyard,"[18] was written in the Building of the Arts. Mandelstam actually bathed at night in the courtyard —there was no waterpipe in the luxurious residence. Water was brought from a spring and poured up to the very edges of a huge keg which stood in the courtyard. A coarse homespun towel which we had brought from the Ukraine found its way into the poem. We always had a liking for homespun country cloth, little homespun rugs, earthenware jars, and now even a glass jar seems something real in comparison with the whitish pink plastic which Akhmatova for some reason called the "immortal veneer," using the term for all nylon and perlon.... Can these new materials become a part of one's home or will they remain "products" forever? I think that even the death of one's household things (something Mandelstam gave a final tribute to in an essay of 1922) will become a part of the idea of the twentieth century.

"I bathed myself at night in the court-yard" is a short poem. It came alone and at some point was drowned out by others which followed it. Its material is only partly reflected in one which follows it chronologically ("To some winter, arak and blue-eyed punch"),[19] and it did not become the nucleus of the cycle. In a foreign land, and Georgia was a foreign land in spite of Mandelstam's love for the "black sea," poems were destined to fade away. On the other hand, these twelve lines contain an incredibly compact statement of the new attitude of a matured man, and the elements that make up this new attitude are specified: conscience, misfortune, cold, the truthful and terrible earth with its severity, truth as the basis of life, death—the purest and most unambiguous thing given us, and the coarse stars in the heavenly firmament.... For Mandelstam the sky has never been the dwelling place of God, because he felt too clearly His existence outside of space and time. In his work one very rarely encounters the heavens as a symbol, perhaps only in the line, "That the earth cost us ten heavens."[20] And typically these are empty heavens, the edge of the world; and the task of man is to bring life to them by making them commensurate with the work of his hands—a cupola, a tower, a gothic arch. For Mandelstam architecture is not only one of the arts but the assimilation of one of the greatest gifts received by man—that of space, of three-dimensionality. From this comes the appeal not to feel the burden of three-dimensionality as the Symbolists did, but to free it, fulfilling its earthly purpose, to live joyfully and build in this three-dimensional world. The architect says: "I build—that means I am right."[21]

Mandelstam felt space even more strongly than time which he imagined as the governor of human life ("Time cuts me like a coin"[22]) and also as a measure of verse. Time—a century—is history, but man is passive in his relationship to time. His activity develops in space, which he must fill with things and make his home. Architecture is the most distinct trace a person can leave in this world, and consequently it is the pledge of immortality.

In Christianity there is a call to activity —for instance, in the parable about the talents—in distinction from Buddhism and the theosophical currents as well as the pantheistic currents which had conquered minds at the beginning of the century. The Symbolists underwent a powerful influence of the East (in part through Schopenhauer, who was popular in their circles), and the revolt of the Acmeists against them was by no means only literary, but, to a significant degree, also philosophical. Almost all of the Symbolists to some degree or other were striving for a modification of Christianity; they called for a union of it first with antiquity, then with paganism. One of the fashionable themes of the twenties was pre-Christian Rus', in which

Gorodetsky played a role. (Khlebnikov, who was enthusiastically received by Vyacheslav Ivanov, built his fantastic mythology on this very thing.) The Acmeists—individually completely different poets with completely different poetics—united and rebelled against the Symbolists over the "lamp inherited from our ancestors." In essence Futurism had no deep disagreements with the Symbolists. They only completed the business begun by the Symbolists, and they were exceptionally well received and even adopted by the Symbolists. Far more complicated was the case of the Acmeists. Moreover, when speaking about the Acmeists one must immediately exclude Gorodetsky, who had been attracted by Gumilev for "tactical reasons," because Gumilev was afraid to appear with green youth, and so he sought at least one person with a "name." And at that time Gorodetsky was a universal favorite, Blok's "sunny lad," and he was seriously considered the hope of Russian poetry. Zenkevich and Narbut were also people who happened along more or less by chance and who were connected with the original three Acmeists only by friendship.

Mandelstam's worldview was formed very early. Its basic principles had already appeared in the essay "The Morning of Acmeism," which he proposed as a manifesto of the new movement. Gorodetsky and Gumilev disavowed it; Akhmatova always supported Mandelstam. In her early youth she probably did not understand at all what he wanted, but in her mature years she shared the position of this article completely. Mandelstam continued this same tack in the essay "Scriabin and Christianity" (or "Pushkin and Scriabin"), read as a paper at the "Religious-philosophical Society" and preserved only in fragments. In the essays of 1922 the same questions are touched upon, but the very word Christianity had fallen under the censor's total ban and is not used further in essays.

In the poems of 1922-33 Mandelstam again drifted toward apprenticeship, having felt the new voice while still in Tiflis: "What kind of ransom should be paid for apprenticeship to the universe so that the black slate pencil be guided (trained) for firm and instant writing...."[2][3] This is a rough draft of the

"Slate Pencil Ode" through which the theme of apprenticeship passes latently. With Mandelstam, as most likely with many poets, there were two periods of apprenticeship. The first period is one of apprenticeship/training. In Mandelstam's case, in my opinion, it falls in the middle of *Stone* with the poems "Petersburg Stanzas," "Cinematograph," and the poems about sport, of which only "Tennis" went into the book. The second and decisive period of apprenticeship is the one in which the poet seeks his place among the living and dead "masters and managers of poetic material."

Pushkin gave Salieri a monologue about training or the first stage of apprenticeship ("I made craft the pedestal of art"), and one of the reasons for Mandelstam's attraction to Salieri lies in this. Every craft was dear to Mandelstam because the craftsman makes utensils, fills and domesticates the world. Mandelstam once had to express the idea of beauty, and he expressed it through art: "Beauty is not the whim of a demigod but the rapacious eye of a simple joiner...."[24] Furthermore, Mandelstam could not help appreciating the "obedient, dry dexterity" which Salieri imparted to his fingers, as the "good ear" indispensible not only to a musician but also to a poet. Finally, Salieri is a toiler, and during the whole process of creation of a thing every artist is inclined to emphasize most of all the aspect of labor. After all, it is specifically labor which depends upon the will of the artist, on his inner concentration and almost ascetic "selflessness...." In a period when Mandelstam staked his whole bet on the hardness of man, on his strong-willed purposefulness and unwavering character, he obviously had to take the side of the ascetic Salieri and not the diffuse Mozart.

The attraction for Salieri is evoked also by an aversion to the Mozart of the "little tragedy." Pushkin, who had singled out a type of artist who lives by divine inspiration alone without the slightest participation of the intellect and labor (an "idle reveler," one of the "idle fortunate"), a type which was foreign to him and inconceivable in its purest form, made him a dreamer with a vague, romantic vocabulary. Here is the kind of explanatory introduction which Mozart makes before he sits down at the piano: love ("not too intense, just a bit"), a beauty, and "suddenly a sepulchral vision, a sudden gloom or something like that...." This romantic contour is emphasized to an even greater degree in the words of Mozart when he lists himself and Salieri among the elect, the idle fortunates and priests of the beautiful. Here Pushkin separated his Mozart from himself infinitely, and each word in this response ran directly counter to Mandelstam. He hated the position of the elect, and all the more that of the priesthood so characteristic of the Symbolists and so well expressed by Berdiaev (he was close to the Symbolists in his cult of his own aristocratism, fastidiousness and scorn of the simple life). The elitist position of the Symbolists furthered the work of enlightenment which they carried on, but it led to a natural rejection among the younger generations. Those poets I knew not only did not feel themselves to be the elect, but they respected people of the "real" professions no end. This one particular complaint of Mandelstam means a great deal: "Who am I? Not a real stone mason, not a roofer, not a shipwright: I am a double-dealer with a dual soul —I am friend of the night, I am vanguard of the day...."[25] Akhmatova dreamed of being a literary critic, a woman, simply a wife, pouring out tea at a neat table. And on one occasion Pasternak told about a young lady, a secretary, who had given him stupid advice which he, of course, had followed; he had not been able not to believe her: "After all, she sits at a table," i.e., she is a professional and she deals with real matters.... But I would have liked to have been married to a cobbler most of all: a husband with real work and a wife with shoes... What kind of priesthood is this?... But, nevertheless, each of them insisted that they were laborers too. In "The Morning of Acmeism" Mandelstam maintains that the poet's labor is more complicated even than the labor of a mathematician (it is true that the example of mathematical work which he had was a naive one, but he did not need any other). I can also cite this polemical remark by Akhmatova: "As if this carefree existence were not also work...." Not one of them, including of course both Pushkin himself and even the historical Mozart, would have subscribed to the words of Pushkin's Mozart.

Mandelstam, who was by nature passionate and unfair, without investigating things as he should, judging only from these short conversations, numbered Mozart among the Symbolists and their followers—the Imaginists, Futurists, etc.—and Pushkin's Salieri he turned into a severe and strict master of things. (It seems to me that he substituted Bach for him, remembering the well tempered clavichord as a check of mathematical calculations.) Angered, he did not notice that although Mozart uses the word "priest," the real priest is nevertheless Salieri. In the charming scene with the "violinist," where Mozart has taken on true Pushkinian features, Salieri has suddenly puffed himself up, lost his tragic character, and turned into a priest and a pedant, preserving a lifeless relic. If one has to preserve a holy relic, it follows that it is dead...

Salieri turns art into an idol, and this also draws him close to the priestly estate; but Mozart, as B. Birger has correctly noted, lives, works, and demands no reward for his labor. In contrast, Salieri brings suit against the almighty powers because they did not value his "selflessness" sufficiently. Art and in particular verse really is not what we understood it to be in our youth.

In the essay "Notes on Poetry" (1922) Mandelstam wrote: "Pushkin has two expressions for innovation, one of which is 'so as to fly away later, after exciting a helpless wish in us, children of dust' and the other 'when the great Gluck appeared and showed us new secrets....' " Mandelstam called the innovator of the first type (i.e., the Mozart of the "little tragedy") a seducer. Pushkin probably knew that Gluck reformed opera singing, introducing recitative into it, but it is unlikely that he was speaking about innovation. The very theme of innovation resounded most urgently of all in the Twenties when under the influence of LEF it was proclaimed virtually the sole value and criterion of art. This was a sickness of the time, like chicken pox, and it also ended in peeling. Mandelstam felt this illness early and came out against it with no less furor than against the Symbolists. In this case he called on Pushkin's help and modernized his words: after all, Pushkin speaks not about innovation but about the uniqueness of the artist. An artist is unique to a greater degree than the average person, and Mandelstam understood this perfectly; otherwise he would not have said, "Do not compare—a living being is incomparable...." Akhmatova used to say that a great poet, like a dam, impedes the flow of a river. Pushkin's poems, especially *Onegin,* restricted the possibilities of other poems coming into being for a long time because everyone involuntarily wrote in the same stream. Nekrasov was the first to break through the dam, and later Mayakovsky. Akhmatova saw Mayakovsky's significance in this. In a similar fashion Pasternak "stuck in the throat" of a whole generation of poets. Only Tsvetaeva alone withstood the influence of both Pasternak and Mayakovsky and found her own voice. In these words of Akhmatova I hear the voice of a literary critic, and I cannot especially imagine poetry as the flowing of a river. After all, there is continuity in a flow (movements and schools as Tynyanov imagined them), while poetry lives only as unique voices which echo each other, because "everything existed of old, everything repeats itself again..."[26] A few heavenly songs are sufficient justification for the life of a poet; he never leaves a successor, and everything comes about as in a letter of Mandelstam to Tynyanov: "It has been a

quarter of a century now that I have been running aground on Russian poetry, confusing
important things with trifles, but soon my
verse will merge with it and change something
in its structure and make-up...."

But Mandelstam was capable of rebelling
against Mozart even on account of these "heavenly songs," because the word "heavenly"
used in the meaning "beautiful," can be understood by a partial ear as "not of the here and
now," "otherworldly...." In the revolt against
the Symbolists both Gumilev and Mandelstam
objected especially to the Symbolists striving
here on earth to understand the other world
with the help of symbols. Vyacheslav Ivanov
urged leaving reality for the sake of a more
real (otherworldly) world, and for Berdiaev
all that existed on earth were symbols of a
better life toward which he strove, hoping to
find himself in the kingdom of the spirit as
fast as possible. In his polemical articles Gumilev declared that it is impossible to know the
unknown under any circumstances and that
"all attempts in this direction are immoral..."
Mandelstam compared the Symbolists to an
ungrateful guest "who lives at his host's ex-

pense, uses his hospitality, and meanwhile despises him in his soul and besides that thinks only about how he might trick him." In the same essay ("The Morning of Acmeism") he said: "To exist is the artist's highest self esteem." This means being and remaining in the memory of people here on earth, but after all it is precisely Mozart who exists once he has brought a few heavenly songs here.

Two Sides of the Same Process

Once long ago, perhaps it was while still on Tversky Boulevard at the beginning of the twenties—because only then, after our return from Georgia, would Mandelstam drop in at the meetings of the Union of Poets from time to time to hear what kind of verse they were reading—he returned home after listening to the poets and translators for a long time and said, "I understand: it seems to them that they are flying too, only nothing comes of it..." I too happened to meet people who had all the signs of "flight," but in the end what remained was a pile of dust and a heap of scribbled pages. Evidently "flights" can be fruitful and devasting, genuine and imagined, free and self-willed. The very feeling of "flight" is still no guarantee that valuable poems will appear as a result, and fruitless efforts devastate and stupefy a man. Apparently a poet must know not only how to speak, but also how to be quiet in those instances when the impulse impelling him to create verse is not strong enough. It is much harder for a poet to stop himself, to refuse to work than to immerse himself in it at the first call. Each person who writes verse probably knows that separate lines and even stanzas often flash through the poet's head. It is possible to catch hold of such a "wandering" line or stanza as Mandelstam called them, and bringing one's self round to a sympathetic state of mind, to add something else to it, following the rules of composition, in order to get a poem. Still-born poems come about in this manner. In a period when Mandelstam was not writing poems there were so many wandering stanzas in his head that he did not even begin to write them down. He told me about this when the poems returned, and to my question why he did not try to use these stanzas, he replied, "That would not have been right..." He was not able or did not want to explain why this was "not right." I understood from this conversation what role self-restraint plays for the poet. He must have a powerful controlling apparatus in order to recognize the quality and worth of the impulses.

A poet keeps silent if he has not matured enough for that profound and selfless activity which lies before him. Sometimes this comes about because he has not yet shunned vain activities so that he can feel his profundity, and sometimes because his "soul is waning," as Herzen once said. Mandelstam used to say that poems arise when some sort of event takes place, whether it is good or bad does not matter. This is an attempt to rationally explain profound processes which do not lend themselves to any explanation. In a "waning soul" any event passes by unnoticed and in days of spiritual efflorescence everything is felt as an event, no matter what—a gust of wind, a fallen apple, a cloud, a bird in a cage... And I have also noticed that a poet is ready to create an "event" artificially when the poetic impulse, the "wind of Orpheus," weakens, loses force, comes to nothing... This comes about at the end of a poetic period or "book." An artificial event does not last long, and the wind dies down all the same. It is impossible to call it forth, and it is impossible to protract it for long. On the other hand, when it blows it is impossible to stop it. It is possible and necessary to stop only imaginary impulses.

When speaking about the process of creation the poet cannot do without metaphors and comparisons. A certain chastity prohibits him from penetrating into, or all the more, from analyzing all the moments contained in this act. It is possible that he is not completely aware of what happened to him in the period when the "resonating whole" was being formed. One thing, a feeling of amazement, remains with him; and when speaking about his experience he usually prefers to use figures of speech which were invented before him. Pushkin has two concepts which exist for the designation of the whole process—inspiration and work. Akhmatova used the old word "muse" and often would speak simply of work. Almost everyone who has decided to open his "laboratory" partially (still another conventional idea used for "grounding" creative work) has spoken about the dual nature of creative work. Dostoevsky distinguished two stages in the creation of a thing—the work of a poet and the work of an artist. Was there in such a division an exact understanding of the essence of the work of an artist? Most likely this is simply still another conventional division of the two principles of creative work. In Akhmatova and Mandelstam's conversation these two principles were called "Mozart" and "Salieri," although in fact the "little tragedy" provides no basis for such a generalization. In it Mozart is really the bearer of inspiration alone, but Salieri knows both inspiration and labor. The following words of Salieri prove this: "Perhaps ecstasy will visit me, as well as a creative night and inspiration..." In Pushkin these two are rather vessels of different volume, but in the present essay these two names are used as still another metaphorical designation for the two sides of a single process.

Some information about how a poetic whole arises is scattered through "Conversation about Dante," Mandelstam's most mature and last essay. Speaking about Dante, Mandelstam is without a doubt using his knowledge of the creative process, his own experience; and for this reason the information given by him is at the same time a self-confession. If they are collected and arranged in the necessary order, one can get a general impression about all the stages of the process and define what role the two principles arbitrarily called Mozart and Salieri play in it.

Quickly and immediately qualifying it as too sweeping even though correct, Mandelstam says, "Comedy had a seemingly hypnotic seance as its prerequisite." Hypnosis (inspiration) presupposes a hypnotizer, but he is not named. He is talking about the state of anxiety and tears, including the moment when the "resonating impression of the form" arises. Mandelstam introduced the idea of a "seemingly hypnotic seance" in order to reveal this secret and inexplicable condition by means of a comparison with the more or less known trance which accompanies hypnosis. A comparison with hypnosis permits one to make the following conclusions: this condition does not depend upon the will of the poet, on the contrary, he experiences it as a command from within, as someone's powerful will acting upon him, similar to the prophet of Pushkin's poem ("fulfill my will").[27] From this moment the inner voice begins to sound: the command of the prophet—"take heed."

Mandelstam maintains that "he (Dante) does not introduce one word of his own . . . he

takes dictation, he is a copyist, he is a translator..." A literary critic would not be able to
say this. Only a poet who has known from
his own experience the categoricalness of the
inner voice could say this. From the cited
quote it follows that in poetic work no arbitrariness, no invention, no fantasy is conceiv-
able. All these ideas Mandelstam relegated to
the negative rank: "Dante and fantasy—after
all, the two are incompatible! Shame on you,
French Romantics, wretched *'incroyables'* in
red vests, who slandered Aligieri." Mandelstam
would always talk this way about fantasy, as
if the very word included the epithets "un-
bridled" and "unrestrained," and he absolutely rejected its role in the creative process. Fantasy and invention yield a fictive product—
fiction, literature—but not poetry. It is no accident that the English call literature "fiction," separating it from poetry by this very
designation. To poetry in this sense of the
word belong not only works written in verse
forms, but everything which is genuine in distinction from what is fictive—which can also
assume verse form. There are eras when only
a literary production, fiction, is possible be-

cause the inner voice is smothered and the "soul wanes."

In the "Conversation about Dante" Mandelstam introduced a new idea—the impulse. Essentially this signifies the spirit's movement, but what is crucial is how Mandelstam defines the role of an impulse in the creative process. He emphasizes the impulse, which is basic in meaning and first in time: "A thing comes into being as a whole as a result of a singular differentiating impulse with which it is penetrated." This impulse is called "differentiating" because the whole is not made up of parts but on the contrary, as Mandelstam has shown, parts break off from the whole as if flying out of it.

As a result of the first impulse the "unceasing formative urge" (which Mandelstam attributes to some sort of instinct like the instinct of bees building honeycombs) begins to act. Impulse-formation (after the first impulse, which penetrates the whole thing, follow others which define separate movements, or rather, "transformations" of poetic material) is placed higher by Mandelstam than instinctive form-formation. The impulses are the bearers of sense, and form can be squeezed out of the conception like water out of a sponge only when one requirement is met—that the sponge originally contain moisture. The impulse is also called "magnetized" and equated with longing: "There is no syntax—there is a magnetized impulse, a longing for a ship's poop, a longing for a worm's feed, a longing for an unpublished law, a longing for Florence..." Impulses are articulate and saturated with concreteness insofar as they are equal to the longing or striving for concrete aims or phenomena. Impulses are the Mozartian principle, a confused and longing soul. In the "little tragedy" Mozart pines and longs for death. There has never been a poet who, in spite of the love of life which is characteristic of poets, did not have an impulse for death. Mandelstam had impulses for death in all periods of his poetic career, with their culmination in the poem on the death of Andrei Bely. For Mandelstam the death of an artist is the culminating creative act. Salieri cannot be the creator of things, as Mandelstam had considered in the twenties, because concreteness and material come with impulses and belong to Mozart.

I think there is a recognized similarity between the way an artist builds a thing and the way a man builds his life. After all, all the reversals on the road of life are also defined by impulses, and the road of life preserves its unity and wholeness only in those instances when each impulse is subjugated to the meaning of the whole. We are always ready to yield to a fraudulent impulse and stray from the path, and this is still no great misfortune if one only remembers himself in time and does not pass too far along the false path and does not come to a dead end: "And I follow hard on their heels, unhappy with myself, unknown—both a blind man and a leader..."

In each person there is both a blind man and a leader. It is good if the leader manages to cope with the whims of the blind man. Mozart, who is led by impulses, is a blind man; Salieri, the intellectual principle, is a leader. His role is to control and regulate. No matter how great Mozart—even if it be the historical Mozart, the composer—the leader, algebra, the intellect is indispensable to him. The intellect is never silent in the creation of a work. Quite the contrary, it is sharpened to the limit;

otherwise Mozart, led by impulses and immersed in his secret hearing, could be led astray. Salieri is not only an intellectual but also a volitional principle, and it too is indispensable in all stages of creative work.

Having forgotten about the polemic with the Symbolists, which was already totally irrelevant in the thirties, Mandelstam underscored the Mozartian principle of creativity in "Conversation about Dante." There is only one place where he pointed out, in metaphorical form as always, both sides of the process: " 'He' (Dante) is filled to the brim with a feeling of inexplicable gratitude for that cornucopia of riches which has fallen into his hands (the Mozartian principle)." After all, he has no small task: one must prepare a space for the influx (the idea of "influx"[2 8] is taken from cinema technique; all preparatory work which demands knowledge belongs to Salieri). One must take care that the generosity of the poetic material pouring out does not flow through one's fingers, that it does not disappear through an empty sieve (again concern, i.e., will, means Salieri). Furthermore, Salieri has left a letter, a piece of calligraphy, that is, a final redaction of the text. Salieri is strong in algebra; a work cannot be built on algebra alone, but no creator of things could manage without law or formula.

Mozart and Salieri—these are the two stages of creative work; but they are not separated in time, they are both present continuously, complementing each other. They have a common and indivisible path.

A Secret Freedom

The Mozart of the "little tragedy" does not repudiate Salieri, and he proposes a toast "to the sincere union of Mozart and Salieri, two sons of harmony." He is truly ready for the union and ready for friendship, laying no claim to first place among those he considers to be sons of harmony. The experience of secret hearing forms and transforms a person: petty instincts of pride and self-aggrandizement wither at the root, although this of course does not exclude the "wondrous attacks of self-doubt" at the moment of work. On the other hand, a completed, finished work seemingly falls away from its creator, and he looks at it from aside, noting all its merits and shortcomings with calm, almost indifferent impartiality. Precisely for this reason Mozart could not get angry with the "violinist," and Pushkin knew this. Mozart is friendly and trusting, Salieri is mistrustful. But in each real poet the two co-exist, and it is no accident that Pushkin endowed both with his own characteristics. I. M. Semenko has noticed a connection between these words of Salieri— "To die? I thought: perhaps life will bring me unexpected gifts . . . Perhaps a new Hayden will create a great thing—and I will find delight in it"—and Pushkin's lyrical declaration—*"O friends, I do not want to die,* I want to live in order to think and suffer, and I know that for me there will be delights among sorrows, cares, and troubles: from time to time *I will again revel in harmony,* I will weep tears over my invention..."[29] And on the other hand in his "Epistle to Katenin" Pushkin takes Mozart's position, saying that Katenin offers him not the cup of friendship but a goblet of sweet poison. There are areas in which Mozart and Salieri are indistinguishable—for example, in their passion for harmony. I do not know, for instance, which of them carries on the struggle for the "social dignity and public position of the poet," a struggle which Mandelstam called "Kammerjunkerish and purely Pushkinian." Most likely both take part in this struggle, but perhaps they act by different methods. What sharply distinguishes them one from the other results from "secret hearing."

Not only does Mozart not demand rewards for his work, he is "filled to the brim with inexplicable thankfulness" that such wealth has befallen him. Mozart never forgets that he is unworthy of his gift and that he has never deserved it; and furthermore, he knows perfectly well that a gift is by no means given for merit. This feeling of being unworthy of a gift is characteristic of every poet, because a gift is revealed in secret hearing which does not depend upon the will of the poet, on his efforts and endeavors. It is impossible to become accustomed to secret hearing. One never gets accustomed to a miracle; one may only wonder at it. A poet is always filled with wonder. Most likely it is precisely this wonder which annoys upright people—"the malicious mob stood round him." Wonder seems suspect to the mob: it respects only priests. The miraculous wonder of the young Pasternak was so reflected in his eyes that the literary functionaries reconciled themselves to it for the time-being and left him in peace. Akhmatova masked her wonder with mischief, and when Mandelstam was struck by wonder, he would only have a good time. There was a certain guardedness in Akhmatova because she was always waiting the arrival of verse; but Mandelstam was always caught by surprise, often in the midst of noise and people, and he did not even try to hide anything. Of the three he was the most defenseless.

Wonder never weakens, and it is just this which evokes the fear, which each poet knows well, that the poem which has just been created might turn out to be the last in his life; because it is difficult to await the repetition of a miracle. In every miracle there is a uniqueness. Mandelstam says of unexpected rhythm that "it will never return, or it will return in a completely different form..."

The greater the poet, the sharper his feeling of being unworthy of the gift of wonder and thankfulness. A poet is capable of all sins except one—arrogance. Had Pushkin not felt his gift to be an undeserved good fortune he would not have said of the poet, "Perhaps he is the most worthless of all..."[30] A versifier would never say this because he knows that he is indebted only to himself for his successes. Benediktov amazed his contemporaries in discovering what is called a "device," and he attained great virtuosity in the use of these "devices." Good verse, beautiful verse, pretty verse—all of these are by no means the sign of a real poet. The sign of a real poet is only poetry itself. The "unexpected" in poetry is the vibration of poetry itself and not the unexpectedness of the device. This difference is perfectly precise, but how to tell one from the other, no one knows. Only a few people immediately tell one from the other, and the rest—they are always the majority—are inevitably deceived. Time usually erases the mistakes of contemporaries, but parts of their mirages are preserved in the histories of literature and even in the evaluations of their descendents. It has always been and always will be this way, because it is impossible to find any objective criteria.

Salieri is not among the versifiers in any way. He has studied a craft, but the versifier uses a device. "The first step is difficult and the first road is boring"—only Salieri can overcome them. In antiquity one had to pass a test in order to enter art. The question remains whether a craft is only technique or whether it includes other elements. V. Veisberg asked me bluntly what I meant by craft.[31] The habit of pronouncing the word without thinking hindered me in discovering its meaning. In Veisberg's opinion a craft should be understood as tradition, and I think this is correct. Mandelstam argued that invention in poetry (and, for that matter, in any art and science) yields fruit only in those cases where it goes hand in hand with memory. If we accept the definition given by Veisberg, we can isolate a few of the features which characterize the Mozartian and Salierian sides of the creative process.

A craft is directed towards the past, and an artist like a child passes through three stages, mastering unconditional, conditional, and cultural conventions. I use here terms provided by my long-time friend, the psychologist Vygodsky. Craft consists both of technique and knowledge of harmony and ideas which were discovered by participants in a conversation which was begun before us. Salieri supports the canon and the school; the awakened Mozart looks toward the future, and "he sees in tradition not so much its holy, dazzling side as an object used well with the help of ardent reporting and passionate experimenta-

97

tion." The relations of Mozart and Salieri remind me of the priest and the prophet of the ancient church, which I read about in Frank. The priest, an ecclesiastic, preserves the precepts and legend; but the prophet is a layman and looks toward the future. Salieri submits to necessity; Mozart realizes freedom. These two realms—the past and the future, memory and foresight, freedom and necessity—are mutually intertwined and inseparable. In their totality they yield art and science, history and life...

Necessity is not the constraint and curse of determinism, but the connecting link between different times, a "lamp, inherited from our ancestors," if it has not been trampled upon. Necessity is beautiful when the lamp burns, and it results from a voluntary submission to authority. "But the whole misfortune lies in the fact that in authority—or rather, in authoritativeness—we see only insurance against mistakes, and we simply cannot make sense of that grandiose music of trustfulness, faith, and nuances of probability and believing as subtle as the colors of an alpine rainbow," which flow from an unbiased humility before genuine authority. Necessity becomes an unbearable burden if no light is visible; the connecting link between times is destroyed, and instead of the real past with its deep roots, we get "just yesterday."

A poet lives in his time, and he can never leave it. Like everyone else, he possesses a certain degree of freedom and he is subjected to necessity. There is always poison in the present time: bowing before an imagined authority, substitution of culture-worship for genuine culture, idols and images of the current day and yesterday, petty and great temptations, which he is subjected to every minute. Life passes as a test both for Salieri and for Mozart. For the former this is a renunciation of tradition for the sake of yesterday; for the latter—the rupture of his union with Salieri and the renunciation of his own freedom. Even Pushkin was subjected to this temptation, as soon as he said to himself, "You are a tsar, live alone, walk your free road wherever your free mind leads you."[32]

Sometimes it seems to me that in apocalyptic epochs when all thoughts and feelings of people are judged, it is not harder but easier for a poet to preserve his inner freedom, compared to peaceful periods when not coercion but indifference or praise act upon him, "Because a slave is free when he has overcome fear..." When a slave overcomes his fear in the face of naked coercion, he feels his inner freedom with greater keenness than people who are externally free, who essentially are not threatened by anything. In his youth Mandelstam said, "I stand here, I cannot do otherwise."[33] Inner freedom has been preserved by those who knew what they were standing on. A poet cannot live a double life without renouncing poetry and the gift of secret hearing. This is accounted for by the demand for unity which Mandelstam speaks of in his essay "Pyotr Chaadaev." This unity is a result of the "joining of the moral and rational elements," which also gives a personality a special staunchness.

Inner freedom, which is often spoken of in reference to poets, is not simply freedom of will or freedom of choice, but something different. The paradox of inner freedom is that it depends upon the ideas to which it is subjugated and upon the depth of this subjugation. I cite Mandelstam's words about Chaadaev, "The idea organized his personality, not only his mind; it gave this personality structure, architecture. It subjugated to itself all of this personality without exception, and as a reward for absolute submission it granted it absolute freedom." The prophet to whom it was said, "Fulfill my will," is the bearer of this absolute inner freedom. In precisely this same way Frank says that only by serving God and subordinating oneself to Him does man find himself and realize his freedom. Only one who has lost his soul can save it.

I can define my own role in life this way: I was a witness to poetry. In the years of tribulation first one, then another would be seized by dumbness. The reasons for dumbness were various: horror, fear, an attempt to justify what was taking place, or even an intensified interest and attention to what was going on around—any of these could become a reason for dumbness, i.e., the loss of oneself. After all, each of these conditions bears witness to the weakening of the basic idea, to the destruction of spiritual wholeness. Nor was indifference pernicious to a lesser degree.

The only thing which could save one was the knowledge of poetic rightness, and it is attained by a full awakening during which the poet sees all, knows all, and without looking back carries on his business "against the grain" of time and the epoch.

Rough Drafts

We always deal with the finished work, and until recently we were hardly interested in how it comes into existence, what the creative process is and through what stages it passes. Concerning the finished work we have only one criterion—verification by time, i.e., verification of its durability: if it has not disintegrated that means it is good. However, it is not known what period is necessary for such verification and how the reality of a work is purged of time. Even long lived works can lose their reality and then be resurrected again, depending upon the necessities of the current period; but be that as it may, it is precisely these that make up the gold reserve of humanity. There are works that bring order into our vain world; but in our great ingratitude we forget this, and from time to time we renounce humanity's greatest divine inspirations, saying that it is time to put an end to prejudices, and then we pay a huge price for this, not even suspecting what we are paying for. The human race is always the same: if you give a man a chance to live his life again, he will make all the mistakes that he made the first time, and it would be the same for history, only the mistakes and crimes would be even more terrible.

But as for a work's formation, the testimony of those who made them has always been the same, and the reaction of their listeners has always been the same: the miracle evokes the mockery and scorn of the rationalists, the intellectual principle is mocked by those who bank on miracles, and the majority lets everything that is said pass by its ears. And although our age has not abolished all these arguments and mutual mockery, nevertheless, it is just at the present that a certain interest in the artist and his thoughts about his work has appeared. And although the cursory attention of witnesses, contemporaries and descendants has remained invariable—still, skimming the surface of the work, they occasionally pose the question of how it appeared and why it had not been noticed earlier.

Mandelstam called a completed work a "literality," the calligraphic product which is left as a result of the performer's impulse. The reader resurrects the work anew: "In poetry the only important thing is the *performing* understanding—which is not passive, which does not reproduce or paraphrase." He proposed reading Dante "with arms waving and with absolute conviction," as if moving to an "active sphere of poetic material." In essence, the whole "Conversation with Dante" is the result of such a reading in which the track of the original impulse shines through what has been formed, through the finished text. Mandelstam complained that the rough drafts of Dante had not been preserved: "The preserving of rough drafts is a law for the preservation of the energetics of the work." But he still felt the energetics through the finished text: "Rough drafts are never destroyed..." In other words, dreaming about how one might look into the rough drafts, he wanted to reconstruct the movement of poetic thought, how it led the poet astray, what he had to renounce, and how he straightened out his path. In the "Conversation about Dante" Mandelstam compares the "transformation of poetic material" to an airplane which designs and produces new ships while in flight. "The

105

assembly and launching of these technically in-conceivable new ships which are produced during flight is not an additional and alien function of the airplane in flight, but is a most indispensable aspect and part of the flight itself; and it is no less a prerequisite to the possibility and safety of the flight than maintenance of the steering gear or a con-stantly running motor." It is precisely these airplanes flying one out of the other which guarantee wholeness and unity of movement. The following auxiliary comparison describes the track that poetic thought takes. Rough drafts would show how the airplane launched in flight suddenly stops and serves as the be-ginning of a separate flight—for a book of lyrics this would be a new poem. Sometimes the airplane launched first yields a movement that immediately bifurcates. The movement stops on one of the paths, and the poet, after guiding the first airplane to its goal, returns to the first which has stopped and guides it to its destination. Other airplanes participate only in the flight of the first airplane, and having accomplished their task they disappear. It is precisely the rough drafts which could reveal all these movements and tracks, but in fact by no means everything reaches paper: the greater part of the work is accomplished in the mind without being written down. Separating the Mozartian principle from the Salierian is quite difficult, but, nevertheless, from time to time it is possible: these two types of work are not separated in time. If a poet were to first create a work and then make corrections in it (as many imagine poetic work), Salieri would turn into something like an editor. But nothing of the kind takes place: Salieri participates continuously in a work's formation. In the process he selects, collects, discards and organizes, from time to time mocking Mozart. Mandelstam's Salieri eternally teased Mozart, the secret-hearer, and mocked lines in flight, still fresh. Sometimes a line, a stanza and even a whole poem would not yield to derision and was preserved in spite of the mocker, yet something was missing. A rough draft, of course, is a self-commentary, and I never cease to grieve over the piles of rough drafts which disappeared wholesale.

In "Conversation about Dante" Mandelstam spoke with wonder of the work of the sculptor: "The chisel removes only the excess, and the sculptor's rough draft leaves no material traces . . . the phasic quality itself of the sculptor's work corresponds to a series of rough drafts. . ." There is only one art where all the stages of a work are preserved and participate, little by little, in the finished work—this is painting. Each layer and each dab, applied at any moment of the formation of the work and even removed by the palette-knife, shines through, works, acts, participates in the whole through all the dabs, layers, and shadings laid on it. Perhaps it is for just this reason that craftsmanship, knowledge of material, craft-tradition play such a role for a painter. A painter without technical ability is inconceivable; technical ability can turn a poet into a versifier, and poetic speech itself is "infinitely raw, more unfinished, than so-called conversational speech." This means that in poetry everything is said anew, as if for the first time; and there are far fewer frozen phrases and word combinations than in conversational speech.

In the art of the painter, in which everything is always being revivified and schools and movements have such significance, the relationship of the two principles—Mozart and Salieri—is slightly different, and the relationship with the object takes shape differently. In the choice of the object (of any kind) the artist always finds himself, his own "I," and this is not a mirror reflection but something quintessential. It seems to me that there are two basic Mozartian moments in the work of a painter: the differentiating impulse in the principle itself when the object is discovered, and a second at the end, when some sort of unifying takes place as, for example, the last shaded layerings of ikon painting. The choice of the object corresponds to the moment "of the resonating impression of the form" but the last, unifying impulse a painter has is expressed far more acutely than in a poet because the latter's rough drafts have disappeared and remain only on paper, and in the case of the former, they participate in the finished work. Is this not why serialization is possible for a painter, because he cannot completely reassemble all his elements within the bounds of the one canvas, while a poet sometimes does not leave a single word of the original variant in his completed work.

For painters "school" in the literal sense of the word plays a big role, but not independent instruction—apprenticeship—as it does for the poet. Painters develop later than poets, and they live longer. Often a painter's best works are done in old age. The self-education of a painter consists in his learning to master his impulses. I do not know if there are poets who work systematically every day. I think that a poet's work is always irregular and spontaneous, while a painter's is unthinkable without uninterrupted work. In other words, a poet masters his impulse to a lesser degree than a painter.

A painter often switches off the impulse in order to give time for preparatory work which is purely technical but in which there is also a Mozartian element. A characteristic example of such work is the colored constructions, neutral in texture, in Matisse and in the Russian ikon, which have only one role—to be translucent. In painting there can exist works built on technical ability alone; these are standard productions which belong to a good school. They are made totally using other people's experience and are not a miracle, but they preserve something of the miracle. In the fine arts an element of craftsmanship exists independently and creates works; in poetry this is always poison or "journalistic poetry."

The poet is a much rarer phenomenon than an artist because his work has to be unexpected, and the value of the unexpected depends upon the depth of his personality. A painter can renounce unexpectedness and work canonically.

Every impulse is translated into motor activity, into movement. In a painter this activity is expressed in movements of his hand, which can reach automatism. There is not any automatism in the art itself; it occurs only in the movements of the hand. A painter can sometimes not notice separate movements, just as we are not aware how articulation takes place when we are speaking.

One could suppose that if the poet is a hearer of secrets, then the painter is a seer of secrets, but I think that both the poet and the painter become a part of the work with all their being, both spiritual and physical, and they participate in it with all their talents and feelings. But I am a witness only of poetry, I have had to view painting from aside. And the things that I have said about the painter are only my suppositions, not my observations. I cannot answer for them in essence.

Secret hearing and secret sight, if they exist, are by no means products of the subconscious as the rationalists would have it. Explaining such phenomena by the subconscious, we exchange man's highest spheres for incomparably more primitive ones. Something from the subconscious can break through in the work, but it is based not on the "id," as it is customary to call this sphere, but on the pure, genuine, deepened and widened "ego." "Id" is the man from the "underground" inside a man, and only a victory over him yields the genuine art which the ancients not without reason linked to catharsis, cleansing. It has crossed my mind that those to whom it seems that "they fly, only nothing comes of it for them," are really drawing on that which has been "dislodged," on the "id."

In the same way no art nor cognitive activity is the result of sublimation in which there is an element of self-emasculation, of rejection of any part of one's own being, but emasculation has produced nothing either in art or in science. For the ancient ikon painter periods of trial and abstinence, of fasting and prayer by no means meant a transformation of one kind of energy into another, but only self-restraint and quiet in which the inner voice is better heard. In religious art this is personal contact with God before the last synthesizing impulse. And in every art the attainment of harmony is the highest function of man, in which he draws near to what our God-forsaken century longs for.

Footnotes

1. *Za takuiu skomoroshinu,*
   Otkrovenno govoria,
   Mne svintsovuiu goroshinu
   Zhdat' by ot sekretaria...

2. The Russian is *ptichka Bozh'ia,* referring to the sixteen-line song in trochaic tetrameter from Pushkin's narrative poem *The Gypsies.*

3. The Russian word is a neologism—*bukvennitsa.*

4. From Anna Akhmatova's *A Poem without a Hero,* Part I, Afterword:

   Vse v poriadke: lezhit poema
   I, kak svoistvenno ei, molchit.
   Nu, a vdrug kak vyrvetsia tema,
   Kulakom v okno zastuchit...

5. From Akhmatova's poem "In 1940" ("V sorokovom godu"):

   Uzh ia li ne znala bessonnitsy
   Vse propasti i tropy,
   No eta kak topot konnitsy
   Pod voi odichaloi truby...

6. From Pushkin's poem "The Prophet":

   Dukhovnoi zhazhdoiu tomim
   V pustyne mrachnoi ia vlachilsia . . .

   Kak trup v pustyne ia lezhal.

7. The Russian words are *predpesennaia trevoga.*

8. From *Eugene Onegin,* VIII, 58:

115

> *I dal' svobodnogo romana*
> *Ia skvoz' magicheskii kristall*
> *Eshche ne iasno razlichal.*

9. In Russian: *Zvuchashchii slepok formy.*

10. From V. Khodasevich's poem "Psyche! My poor..." ("Psikheia! Bednaia moia..."):

> *Prostoi dushe nevynosim*
> *Dukh tainoslyshan'ia tiazhelyi.*
> *Psikheia padaet pod nim.*

11. The first four lines of an untitled poem from Mandelstam's first book, *Stone (Kamen').*

> *Slukh chutkii parus napriagaet*
> *Rasshirennyi pusteet vzor,*
> *I tishinu pereplyvaet*
> *Polnochnykh ptits nezvuchnyi khor.*

12. From Mandelstam's "Octaves" [*Vos'misti-shiia, II* ("Liubliu poiavlenie tkani...")]. See Osip Mandel'shtam, *Sobranie sochinenii* (Inter-Language Literary Associates, 1967), I, 198:

> *I tak khorosho mne i tiazhko,*
> *Kogda priblizhaetsia mig—*
> *I vdrug dugovaia pastiazhka*
> *Zvuchit v bormotaniiakh moikh...*

13. From an unpublished rough draft of Mandelstam:

> *A na gubakh kak chernyi med gorit i muchit*
> *Pamiat'. Ne khvataet slova—*
> *Ne vydumat' ego: ono samo gudit,*
> *Kachaet kolokol bespamiatstva nochnogo...*

14. First two lines of Akhmatova's "In 1940":

> *No ia preduprezhdaiu vas,*
> *Chto ia zhivu v poslednii raz...*

15. The opening lines of an untitled poem in *Stone*:

> *Otchego dusha tak pevucha,*
> *No tak malo milykh imen,*
> *A mgnovennyi ritm—tol'ko sluchai,*
> *Neozhidannyi Akvilon?*

16. The Russian word is *poryv.*

17. From Akhmatova's *A Poem without a Hero,* Part I, Chapter 3:

> *A po naberezhnoi legendarnoi*
> *Priblizhaetsia ne kalendarnyi—*
> *Nastoiashchii Dvadtsatyi Vek.*

18. First line of an untitled poem, Mandel'shtam, *Sobranie sochinenii,* I, 96.

> *Umyvalsia noch'iu na dvore...*

19. First line of an untitled poem, Mandel'shtam, *Sobranie sochinenii,* I, 96.

> *Komu zima, arak i punsh goluboglazyi...*

20. The last line of Mandelstam's "The Twilight of Freedom" ("Sumerki svobody") in his collection *Tristia:*

> *Chto desiatki nebes nam stoila zemlia.*

21. A well known line from Mandelstam's essay "The Morning of Acmeism."

22. Last line of Mandelstam's "Horse-shoe Finder" ("Nashedshii podkovu") in *Tristia:*

Vremia srezaet menia kak monetu.

23. Unprinted rough draft of Mandelstam's "Slate Pencil Ode" ("Grifel'naia Oda"):

Kakoi by vykup zaplatit'
Za uchenichestvo vselennoi,
Chtob chernyi grifel' povesti (priuchit'),
Dlia tverdoi zapisi mgnovennoi...

24. Lines 7 and 8 of Mandelstam's poem "The Admiralty" ("Admiralteistvo") in *Stone:*

...krasota ne prikhot' poluboga,
A khishchnyi glazomer prostogo stoliara.

25. Eighth stanza of the "Slate Pencil Ode."

Kto ia? ne kamenshchik priamoi,
Ne krovel'shchik, ne korabel'shchik:
Dvuruzhnik ia, s dvoinoi dushoi.
Ia nochi drug, ia dnia zastrel'shchik...

26. Line 23 of Mandelstam's poem "Tristia."

Vse bylo vstar', vse povtoritsia snova...

27. Pushkin's words here and in the following quote from "The Prophet" are: "...ispolnis' voleiu moei..." and "Vnemli..."

28. The Russian word is *naplyvy.*

29. From Pushkin's lyric "Elegy" ("Bezumnykh let ugasshee vesel'e"), 1830.

30. From Pushkin's poem "The Poet" (1827).

31. The Russian word is *remeslo.*

32. From Pushkin's "To a Poet" ("Poetu"):

Ty tsar', zhivi odin dorogoi svobodnoi.
Idi, kuda tebia vlechet svobodnyi um...

33. "Zdes' ia stoiu—ia ne mogu inache..." The first line of an untitled poem in *Stone.* It is a direct translation of Luther's words, "Hier stehe ich—ich kann nicht anders," which stand as the epigraph to this poem by Mandelstam.